Original title:
I Thought I Had It Figured Out...

Copyright © 2025 Creative Arts Management OÜ
All rights reserved.

Author: Amelia Montgomery
ISBN HARDBACK: 978-1-80566-006-4
ISBN PAPERBACK: 978-1-80566-301-0

Whispered Secrets of the Lost

In the garden of dreams, I planted a scheme,
But weeds of confusion made it a meme.
With a map drawn in crayon, I started my quest,
Only to trip on my shoelace – what a jest!

I aimed for the stars, with a rocket of hopes,
But forgot to check if I could fly with ropes.
The compass was spinning, like a dancer on air,
Pointing me south when I wanted to flare.

Magic wands waved, as I conjured a plan,
To bake up a fortune, but burned the whole pan.
With laughter and giggles from my haphazard tale,
I learned life's a circus, and I'm the main fail!

In the end, I proclaimed, with a belly of laughs,
It's the journey that's funny, not the outcome class.
So here's to the mishaps, the blunders, the fun,
I'd rather be lost than not get it done!

Whispering Doubts in Twilight

In the twilight glow, I tried to see,
A map of life laid out for me.
But each direction was a twisty jest,
Each step I took was just a test.

With stars above, I made my claim,
To conquer doubts and win the game.
Yet every turn, I found a snag,
A sock in hand, instead of swag.

The Mirage of Understanding

I reached for wisdom, shiny bright,
But grasped at air, oh what a sight!
Thought I was clever, sharp as a tack,
Turns out my brain is on a snack!

I climbed a hill to gain some sense,
But ended up behind a fence.
Seeking truth with glee and cheer,
But the truth was hiding, oh dear, oh dear!

Chasing Shadows of False Wisdom

I chased the shadows as they danced,
In wisdom's trap, I lost my chance.
Thought I could tango, lead the way,
But tripped on wisdom, went astray.

Each nugget of truth a shiny lure,
But behind each one, a wild detour.
I laughed and stumbled, full of cheer,
A jester's role, it seemed quite clear!

A Map with No Destination

In hand, a map, all crumpled and torn,
It promised places yet to be worn.
I followed the lines with great delight,
Only to find a cat with might!

The compass spins, oh what a joke,
Each point I seek leads to a poke.
With every step, I question the rout,
Perhaps the fun is in the shout!

In the Wake of Misguided Paths

I danced with plans all laid out,
But stumbled on a stubborn route.
Maps conspired, in jest they laughed,
And still I clutched my endless draft.

The road ahead, a winding jest,
With squirrels plotting for a quest.
Each turn betrayed my guiding star,
Yet here I am, a foolish czar.

Laughter echoes in the wild,
As logic plays the wayward child.
With every misstep, joy abounds,
In chaos, silly fortune found.

So here I giggle, take a seat,
In life's grand play, the cast's repeat.
For every twist, a jest or two,
In misguided paths, who knew we grew?

When the Compass Spun Wildly

The compass points just never stay,
A tango gone awry today.
North becomes a friendly foe,
While south says, 'Hey, let's take it slow!'

With every spin, I laugh aloud,
My GPS has joined the crowd.
It tells me left, then tells me right,
The world's a dizzying delight.

I seek a path that's straight and true,
But all I get is silly view.
Landmarks pop up like old friends,
As certainty so quickly bends.

So here I waltz with compass woes,
In circles like a garden hose.
And in the mess of lost and found,
A merry spin is all around!

Certainty's Fragile Mirage

With confidence, I strode ahead,
Yet doubts invaded all I said.
A stone-cold plan turned soft as air,
Like cotton candy unaware.

I set my sights on goals so bright,
But didn't see the slip of night.
The vision blurred, the humor flowed,
As clarity took an off-road load.

The mirage danced just out of reach,
A lesson life was here to teach.
With every step, I chuckle wide,
For bliss is found when lost in pride.

Through fantasies of grand designs,
Reality scribbles funny lines.
In fragile dreams, I find my cheer,
Laughter thrives where doubts appear!

A Tapestry of Unanswered Questions

Threads of thought entwined with glee,
As questions flit like bumblebees.
What's next? Who knows? I grin instead,
A tapestry by jesters spread.

With every knot, a puzzle grows,
In laughter woven, truth bestows.
Every twist and silly turn,
Inquiring minds, these lessons learn.

What's for dinner? Do I need shoes?
Should I dance, or just sing blues?
In whimsy's heart, I find my road,
Amidst the questions, light bestowed.

So let them swirl, those thoughts perplexed,
In jests and giggles, I feel blessed.
My finest moments, they come out plain,
In a tapestry stitched with joy and rain!

The Facade of Understanding Shattered

I wore a mask of wisdom, bright,
But tripped on logic, what a sight!
With every answer, confusion grew,
Like a clown car with more to strew.

The experts spoke with such great flair,
Yet left me dizzy, gasping air.
They mixed their metaphors with grace,
And puzzled looks adorned my face.

Moments of Doubt in the Light

In daylight's glow, I swear I knew,
The tricks and rules of life's big zoo.
But shadows danced with cheeky grins,
As sanity tossed out the bins.

The sun shone bright, yet still I fumbled,
With questions deep, my brain just stumbled.
Is two plus two always a four?
Or could it be a secret door?

Crossroads of Conjecture and Reality

At crosswalks filled with thought and jest,
I pondered which way was the best.
Left took me where the wild things lay,
Right had the ice cream truck at bay.

The signs were blurry, all a blur,
Each step I took just made me stir.
With every answer, more would sprout,
Like weeds that grow where fun's about.

A Puzzle Missing Its Pieces

My life's a puzzle, or so they say,
But half the pieces just won't play.
The corner's missing, it's quite a mess,
Like trying to fit socks in a dress.

With colors bright but edges rough,
I scratched my head, this game's too tough!
But laughter rang in every gap,
As I enjoyed my whimsical hap.

The Fragile Architecture of Assuredness

I built a tower made of dreams,
With blocks of plans and wild schemes.
But watch it wobble, watch it sway,
A breeze of doubt takes it away.

I plastered walls with confidence,
Yet crumbled bricks made recompense.
A ceiling high of hopes so bold,
But down it crashed, a sight to behold.

Blueprints drawn with pencil lead,
Forgot to check the space ahead.
My grand design, so neat and spry,
Turns out it's just a chicken pie.

Still, I laugh through the wreckage found,
For in the mess, new dreams abound.
A comedy in every miscue,
In fragile plans, the laughter grew.

Dance of the Unforeseen

I waltzed through life with pointed toes,
Each step carefully, as everyone knows.
But then my shoe flew off my foot,
And in a twist, I lost the groove.

Chassé forward with no retreat,
I spun and tripped on my own feet.
The dance floor laughed, it gleamed in glee,
As I performed a new routine for free.

A partner joined, with two left shoes,
Our tango turned to a comical muse.
We twirled and stumbled, oh what a sight,
In this chaotic, joyful flight.

So here's my dance, a spoofing spree,
Who knew the mishaps felt so free?
Embrace the laughs, take my hand wide,
In the dance of life, just enjoy the ride.

In the Heart of Confusion

I set my sights on what to do,
A map of thoughts, a grand debut.
Yet every turn led me astray,
In circles round, I lost my way.

With GPS that had a laugh,
It took me down a broken path.
A shortcut promised, so divine,
Led straight to someone's laundry line.

I asked for help, a friendly face,
He pointed right—oh, what a grace!
But somehow left, I did a twirl,
Now I'm lost in a bagel swirl.

Confused but happy, I munch and chomp,
As life unfolds with every rom-com.
And in this haze, I've come to see,
The heart of laughter sets me free.

The Unwritten Chapter of Discovery

I opened up my blankest page,
Hoping wisdom jumps from the cage.
But scribbles danced and words all fled,
The plot turned silly, a clown instead.

My pen took flight, a bird gone wild,
Each thought a prank, no good or mild.
Characters flipped, they changed their tunes,
From noble knights to wacky loons.

The plot thickens well, like a stew,
A side-splitting laugh, that much is true.
When chaos reigns in a story untold,
Adventure awaits, bright and bold.

So here I sit, with pages spun,
In the unwritten, the chaos is fun.
Each twist and turn, a comedic play,
In the chapter of life, I'll find my way.

Disillusionment's Quiet Melody

Woke up one day, plans in my hand,
Coffee spilled coffee, it's out of demand.
The map said 'straight,' but I took a turn,
Turns out my compass still has to learn.

Thought I was slick, dancing with fate,
But now I'm just tripping; can't catch a break.
The road signs are laughing, or so it seems,
Chasing my shadow with grander dreams.

Navigating the Fog of Assumptions

Put on my glasses to see the clear route,
Turned out they're smudged; what's that about?
Thought I was wise, a wizard of sorts,
Now I'm just bumping into fictional forts.

With clouds of confusion, I'm swirling around,
All roads lead to nowhere, it's quite profound.
Each step feels bold, but what have I found?
Socks and old sandwiches lay on the ground.

Unspoken Truths and Untold Stories

Got a degree in making it right,
Yet here I am, lost in the night.
Conversations get tangled like headphones do,
Every nod I give leads to something askew.

Jokes turn to riddles, I can't comprehend,
Saying 'yes' too much, I can't find the end.
Truths I forgot, smothered by cake,
Who knew my stability was such a mistake?

The Journey Beyond Expectations

Packed my dreams in a suitcase, so fine,
But the zipper broke open—it stepped out of line.
I pictured sedans and luxurious views,
Instead, I'm driving a car with broken shoes.

Thought I was the guide, but what a surprise,
My map is a crayon, with colorful lies.
Destination unknown, but that's quite alright,
Laughing at the chaos that's built my flight.

When the Ground Shook Beneath My Feet

I strutted with confidence, grand and tall,
But fate played a prank; I took a big fall.
My shoes flew off like they had a plan,
I landed in mud, just as I began.

The earth did a jig while I tried to stand,
Laughing around me was the comedy band.
I waved to the crowd, my pride in the dirt,
In the symphony of chaos, I found my new shirt.

My coffee flew high, like a bird from a tree,
As I stumbled and fumbled, what a sight to see!
"Is this meant to be?" I asked in surprise,
While the universe chuckled, oh how time flies.

So here's to the tumbles and slips that we take,
Life's just a circus; we giggle and shake.
In moments of madness, we find sweet delight,
With a whoop and a laugh, we conquer the night.

Reflections on a Shattered Facade

Mirror, mirror, you trickster bright,
You showed me perfection, yet here's my plight.
I tried to be fancy, a true work of art,
But ended up looking like a lopsided tart.

In pursuit of glam, I slipped on some cream,
The cake must have laughed at my fancy dream.
My hair was a tornado, like squirrels in flight,
As I posed with such grace, oh what a sight!

With every reflection, I cringed and I sighed,
Who knew my reflection was such a wild ride?
Each flaw was a gem, each blunder a crown,
In the comedy show, I just couldn't frown.

So here's to the days of the messy and weird,
To laughter and chaos, let no one be feared.
With cracks in our facades, we stumble and cheer,
Embracing the chaos, we find reason to leer.

The Twilight of My Beliefs

Once bright and shiny, my ideals did beam,
Like a paper mache boat in a never-ending stream.
But winds of confusion blew wildly about,
My trust set sail, and it twisted right out.

With certainty drifting like leaves in the breeze,
I laughed with my doubts, who cares about fees?
The universe giggled, I tossed in a wink,
Maybe it's fine, to just float and rethink.

Each truth I held tight turned into sponge cake,
As I mixed up my visions, for goodness' sake!
In twilight's embrace, I stumbled and spun,
What once was a race, was now just pure fun.

So raise up your glasses, let's toast to the night,
For beliefs are but shadows, I'm told we're all right.
In the dance of the unclear, we twirl and we glide,
Finding joy in the questions, all worries aside.

Threads of Certainty in a Woven World

I knitted my plans with yarns of bright hue,
Confidently binding, like I really knew.
But knots in my needles turned tangled and wild,
The sweater I made looked like fashion defiled.

In threads of belief, I pulled and I tugged,
But fabric of life had my verses all mugged.
With each stitch I placed on my woven delight,
I laughed as it morphed into something not right.

The patterns I thought were a masterpiece grand,
Became a mishmash that stumped even the hand.
My grand tapestry now a patchwork of glee,
In a world full of wobbles, it's perfect for me.

So here's to the chaos, the threads out of place,
In the game of existence, I embrace the embrace.
Laughing with yarns, let's unravel and play,
In the fabric of life, we'll weave our own way.

The Fading Echo of Confidence

Once I wore a crown of wit,
With every joke, the laughter hit.
But then my punchlines took a dive,
Like a fish who forgot how to thrive.

I strutted with a grin so bright,
But tripped on air; oh what a sight!
My confidence, a balloon in flight,
Popped by a pin of sheer fright.

I asked my brain for guidance true,
It sent back memes, a funny crew.
A game of chess with no real stakes,
I'm the king, but forgot how to take.

Now I joke about my fall from grace,
Life's a circus, and I'm the base.
A clown with dreams, but laughs win out,
So here we are, and there's no doubt!

Beneath the Surface of Resolve

I stood firm with my head held high,
Determined, I reached for the sky.
But deep within, a whisper crept,
A tickle of doubt that boldly leapt.

I wrote a list of goals to chase,
Then lost it all without a trace.
My resolve slipped like butter on toast,
A breakfast spread I liked the most.

Each plan I made led to a swap,
Like a dancing broom that wouldn't stop.
Twirling chaos in my tidy room,
As I laughed so hard, I welcomed doom!

Yet through the mess, I found a spark,
A funny thought that lit the dark.
Beneath the surface of my dreams,
Who knew life's plan was full of memes!

The Fine Line Between Knowledge and Ignorance

With textbooks stacked like leaning towers,
I felt like Einstein in my powers.
But ask me one simple, silly thing,
And I'll just nod like a puppet on string.

I spout off facts with great aplomb,
Then mix up lizards and a bomb.
A noodle here, a noodle there,
Turns out they're both spaghetti, I swear!

The internet calls me a wiz so grand,
While I trip on words, unsure where I stand.
I'm an expert on cheese, or so it seems,
But ask about milk? Forget those themes!

Each day a puzzle, new and bizarre,
I flip the pieces but never go far.
So here's to ignorance wrapped in delight,
In this circus of facts, I'll be just right!

A Compass with No True North

I bought a compass to find my way,
It spins and dances; what a display!
North is here, or maybe just there,
I follow its lead; whom do I scare?

Each direction feels fresh and new,
Like a chicken trying to bake with a shoe.
I wander as if lost in a maze,
Chasing my tail in a comedic daze.

The sun says east, the moon says west,
It's a contest of who knows best.
I laugh and take it in my stride,
In this journey, I'll enjoy the ride!

So here's to life's wayward twists,
With maps that argue, and charts that insist.
My trusty compass may be a joke,
But it's guiding me, through laughter I'll poke!

When Clarity Began to Blur

There once was a thought in my head,
It sparkled like gold but lay dead.
Plans crumbled like crumbs,
As confusion struck drums.

I crafted a route, with great flair,
But a squirrel stole the map from the air.
Chasing ideas so bright,
I got lost in the night.

A beacon appeared, then it slipped,
I followed a cat that just nipped.
Oh, clarity's lost,
At a bewildering cost.

Now I'm stuck with this riddle, it seems,
Life's puzzles are full of wild dreams.
Each step is a dance,
In a chaotic prance.

Fragments of a Plan Unraveled

In the beginning, dreams shone so bright,
Like a new puppy, ready for flight.
But plans often fade,
Like a jester's parade.

Tangled in strings of my grand design,
I picked up my hopes and they feigned a whine.
With laughter, they twirled,
As my thoughts softly swirled.

A checklist of points, full of joy,
Then a goat chewed the pen of this boy.
No ink left to trace,
These ideas run a race.

So here I stand, crumpled bits in hand,
Grinning like fools in a wacky band.
A mess, yes, it's true,
But I laugh with the crew.

The Map That Led Me Astray

With a map made of jelly, I set out,
To navigate lands full of doubt.
But paths turned and swirled,
As my senses were twirled.

I reached for the stars but hit the ground,
Found a taco stand, now that's profound!
Plans tasted so sweet,
But my feet missed the beat.

Each twist of my fate is a laugh,
A dance with a pie, what a gaffe!
The compass beeps loud,
As I wander unbowed.

Maps that mislead are quite funny,
Like a nutty rabbit with money.
I skip while I roam,
In a land far from home.

Echoes of Confidence Crumbled

In the mirror, I saw a great sage,
With a plan that could certainly engage.
But words turned to cheese,
In the gusty sea breeze.

Confidence strutted like a proud lion,
But tripped on a rock, oh, how it was tryin'.
With chuckles and grins,
It danced with its sins.

The echoes of laughter filled the air,
As wisdom plummeted, unaware.
I found my wit's edge,
On a jellyfish ledge.

So cheers to the blunders we hold,
In a tale that's fantastically told.
With a wink and a giggle,
We all find our wiggle.

The Mystery of Miscalculated Dreams

In tales of gold, I fiercely soared,
Yet tripped on clouds, oh how I roared!
With maps unfolded, hope was high,
Until I lost my way, oh my!

Banana peels on sidewalks grand,
A slip and slide, oh wasn't planned!
Vision clear and bright as day,
But zigzag paths led me astray.

Hopes as big as my grandma's pie,
But then the crust was all awry!
With sprinkles tossed, I missed the cake,
And laughed so hard, my sides did shake.

So here I stand, with dreams in hand,
A jester's cap, my life's unplanned.
Each folly brings a laugh, it seems,
In this circus built of dreams.

Lessons in the Dance of Confusion

Upon the floor, I twirled so neat,
But stepped on toes, oh what a feat!
With two left feet and a spin so wild,
I tangoed like a baffled child.

The music played, a funny tune,
I boogied under the watchful moon.
But every misstep drew some cheer,
As laughter echoed, loud and clear.

In a waltz with fate, I took my chance,
But led my partner to a dance of glance.
With jerky moves and a clumsy sway,
We laughed it off and danced away.

Through dips and spins, my brain did whirl,
But life's a dance, so let it unfurl.
Thus, I embrace the comical mess,
In the waltz of life, I find my bless.

Whispers of Uncertainty's Embrace

In shadows deep, my fears awoke,
As whispers danced, oh what a joke!
The plans I penned, so bold and grand,
Turned into sand in my own hand.

With signs so clear, yet lost like fog,
I chased the dreams like a jumping frog.
A map in circles, zigzagged flight,
Took me to places that felt just right.

In quiet moments, doubts took stage,
Yet laughter bubbled, I turned the page.
The chaos reigned, a comic show,
As I embraced the not-so-slow.

So here I stand, midst laughs and sighs,
With giggles bubbling, I improvise.
In uncertainty, I find my grace,
And dance through life in a messy place.

A Flawed Blueprint for Happiness

With blueprints drawn and angles tight,
I dreamt of joy, a perfect sight.
But builders lost, it seems, the plot,
As joy turned into quite a lot!

I sketched a pool in my backyard,
But found a fishbowl, oh how hard!
My heart was set, the yard was bare,
But soggy shoes got me nowhere.

The kitchen plan, a chef's delight,
Turned into chaos – what a fright!
With bowls a-flying, flour a-cloud,
I"m quite the cook, though not too proud.

Yet through it all, I laugh and sing,
For joy's a jester, it's a funny thing.
With blueprints wild, I'll make my way,
In this flawed map, I'll joyful stay.

Tracing Steps Back to the Unknown

With maps in hand, I sought the route,
Each turn I took led to a pout.
The signs all danced in playful jest,
My compass spun, a fool's request.

With every clue I wrote it down,
Yet somehow ended lost in town.
A dog was my best friend today,
It showed me skies where squirrels play.

Barefoot in the grass, I gleam,
Collecting thoughts like catching cream.
I danced through life, a lark on fire,
Turns out I'm just a random flyer.

So here I am, once more, astray,
The routes I drew have gone to play.
I'm lost for sure, but laughter springs,
In the chaos, joy it brings.

When Blueprints Turned to Dust

In the garage, dreams took flight,
With a hammer and a notion bright.
Plans were made on soggy cheer,
Yet all I built was a shed of fear.

I measured twice, then chopped it once,
My vision shattered, like a dunce.
Each wall decided to lean and sway,
A wonky home for my plans to play.

The roof's a puzzle, a jigsaw mad,
I thought it'd be grand, yet look at that!
Winds now whistle through my dreams,
This structure fuels my giggled screams.

So here I dwell, in bits and scraps,
Among broken dreams and silly maps.
Oh, to design a cozy place,
Where chaos has a warm embrace.

The Storm Beneath a Calm Surface

In coffee cups, I sip my thoughts,
The world is still, but chaos plots.
Beneath my grin, a tempest brews,
Juggling life in mismatched shoes.

The surface gleams, all glossy bright,
Yet, oh, the storms dance out of sight.
I toss confetti at my woes,
And twirl about, while laughter flows.

Clock ticks loud, the chaos sings,
I'm queen of whimsy, with jester's rings.
Pretend it's fine, all in a tower,
Who knew that chaos holds such power?

So here I float, with joy and dread,
A silly smile, a wobbly thread.
Underneath, the waves still play,
But let's just dance, come what may!

On the Edge of Revelation

I stood on cliffs of bright delight,
With dreams that sparkled in the light.
The world around me spun and swayed,
Each thought a game, a merry charade.

Peered over edges, wide-eyed and bold,
Searching for truths, a tale untold.
Yet as I looked, the ground gave way,
Into a pit where sock puppets play.

I tumbled down, a laughing fate,
In this wild ride, I celebrate.
For wisdom hides in silly sights,
With puppets waltzing, and gleeful flights.

So here I am, on the brink of cheer,
With laughter echoing loud and near.
If answers come dressed in wild hues,
Then let's all dance in mismatched shoes!

When Understanding Slipped Through My Fingers

I crafted a plan with utmost glee,
But chaos sat down right next to me.
With a map in hand and a coffee cup,
I tripped on a thought, and spilled it up.

Each answer danced, just out of reach,
Like a no-show cat on a sunny beach.
I wore my wisdom like a brand new shoe,
But it squeaked so loud, it scared off the crew.

My spreadsheets gleamed with colors so bright,
Yet numbers engaged in a boring fight.
I searched for logic in a twisty maze,
Only to find it in a playful haze.

So here I am, with a laugh and a grin,
Telling tales of where I've been.
With lessons learned in a comical way,
Life's punchlines come, but oh, they're cray!

Discovering Pathways in the Dark

With flashlight in hand, I wander about,
In a room full of shadows, filled with doubt.
Every corner I turn leads to sheer surprise,
Where did that sock go? Oh look! A surprise.

I blunder through corridors with flamboyant flair,
Stubbing my toe on a metaphor there.
It whispered softly, 'You'll never get far,'
Yet pointed to moments like rays from a star.

The door that I opened creaked like a grin,
Revealing a riddle that tickled my skin.
Paths laid like spaghetti, all twisted and fun,
I giggled and gasped, "Well, this can't be done!"

In the dance of confusion, I found my delight,
With every wrong turn, the future looked bright.
To stumble in darkness feels oddly profound,
With laughter and giggles, where wisdom is found.

The Ruins of My Certainty

I built my fortress, so strong and so tall,
Each brick laid with answers, ready to brawl.
Yet a pigeon flew by, dropped wisdom in doubt,
And the walls of my certainty crumbled throughout.

My golden trophy of knowing it all,
Turned into jello, a wobbly ball.
Each sagging belief, like a lamp on the blink,
Flickered uncertain, oh, what do I think?

I wore my ideals like a crown on my head,
Until they fell off and danced with the dead.
Now rubble surrounds me, yet laughter, not fear,
Is the compass that guides me with joy ever near.

So here in the ruins, I sip on some tea,
Laughing at all that I once thought was me.
Acceptance has landed, like a feather, not stone,
In the mess of uncertainty, I've truly grown.

A Stream of Questions Without End

Why do ducks have such funny feet?
What makes it feel good to dance on the street?
With a whirl of queries spinning in my head,
   I ponder the ways a cat dreams in bed.

Do clouds ever worry whenever it rains?
And do socks feel lonely when they get stained?
My brain's a circus, full of clowns and jest,
   Feeling curious like a child on a quest.

What makes ice cream a favorite delight?
Why are stars only visible at night?
In the land of confusion, I roam with my pen,
   Asking odd questions again and again.

So I'll chase my thoughts down this whimsical stream,
   Caught in the currents of a madcap dream.
With humor and wonder, I tumble and spin,
In the endless parade where the questions begin.

Lost in the Labyrinth of Certainties

In the maze of my bright ideas,
Every turn leads to more queueing fears.
Logic's a jester, wearing a crown,
While I trip over thoughts spinning down.

Maps of knowledge scribbled in haste,
Every path taken feels like a waste.
Bubble-wrapped wisdom is full of holes,
My GPS lost among laughing trolls.

Adventurous routes designed by a fool,
Roundabouts circling my make-believe school.
With liberty bells that only chime wrong,
I dance to the tunes of confusion's song.

Yet here I stand, in this wacky maze,
Searching for sunshine in a foggy haze.
With laughter as my guide, I'll wade through doubt,
In this wild labyrinth, I'll figure it out!

Beneath the Weight of Assumptions

With a hat full of notions, I march with pride,
Observing the world like I'm a wise guide.
But assumptions are heavy, like bricks on my head,
I trip on the stones of the things that I said.

Dressed in beliefs that don't quite fit right,
I look like a clown at a serious night.
Each laugh that erupts feels like an embrace,
Sometimes it's is hard not to fall on my face.

I take sturdy steps, thinking I'm bold,
Only to find my truths have grown old.
The weight of the world just can't bear the jest,
As I tumble through life, I'll just laugh with the rest.

Oh, the hubris of minds that went on parade,
Every wave of certainty begins to fade.
Through giggles and grumbles, I'll take my cue,
Unwrap the false truths and laugh at the view!

When Clarity Crumbles to Dust

Once clear as day, my plans were a treat,
Now they crumble like candy beneath my feet.
Instructions were written in crayon and whole,
And suddenly logic's escaped on a stroll.

I summoned the answers, but they ran away,
Leaving doubts dancing in full cabaret.
With fog rolling in like a bad magic trick,
I'm leaning back, thinking, 'Was this all a quick flick?'

All the wisdom I gathered in jars on the shelf,
Now spills on the floor, turning me to myself.
I laugh at the mess, what else can I claim?
As dust bunnies whisper and giggle my name.

So here in this riddle, I'll twist like a vine,
Giggling softly at the grand design.
With clarity scattered, I'll dance through the fuss,
Taking joy in the dust while it crumbles to dust.

The Illusion of a Straight Path

In a world of straight lines painted bright,
I wander in circles, searching for light.
My roadmap's a joke, with squiggles and bends,
Leading me back to where nonsense descends.

I stride with conviction, my compass in hand,
But the map from the store was made out of sand.
With every misstep, my confidence rocks,
I laugh as I stumble, it's all in the clocks.

Each twist and each turn just adds to my flair,
Like a cat in a tree, I hang with great care.
The straight path's a myth that makes everyone giggle,
For life is a puzzle that loves to wiggle.

Yet in this wild dance, I find my own beat,
As I strut on this path, however discreet.
Embracing the chaos, I'll play my own tune,
For laughter is light, and my heart's like a balloon!

Fractured Reflections in a Shattered Mirror

In the mirror, there stands a face,
But it's just a mask, oh what a disgrace.
Thought I was suave, a true lady charmer,
Turns out I'm just a clumsy farmer.

With a wink and a grin, I made my play,
But my reflection had other things to say.
Laughter erupted from within my own mind,
Guess it's true, confidence is blind.

Each crack told a tale of whimsical fun,
Of missing the mark when the race had begun.
Shattered beliefs, scattered like confetti,
Maybe next time, I'll keep it less petty.

So here I stand, with wisdom in shards,
Playing hopscotch in my own backyards.
Who knew a mirror could hold such jest?
In the dance of life, it's laughter I quest.

Navigating the Sea of Misconceived Notions

Set sail on a boat made of tinfoil dreams,
Navigating waters of overflowing memes.
Thought I'd catch wisdom with a fishing rod,
But all I hooked were thoughts that were odd.

The compass spun wild, like a top on the floor,
Led me to believe I knew so much more.
But every wave whispered tales of the wrong,
In this ocean of blunders, I just sang my song.

Anchors were heavy with goofy insights,
As the seagulls laughed at my outrageous flights.
Flotsam and jetsam of goofy decisions,
Waves washed away all my clear visions.

Though maps were drawn in whimsical clouts,
Turns out, the sea's filled with surprising shouts.
With laughter as my life raft afloat,
I'll navigate folly, and still be the goat.

When Certainty Met the Unexpected

Certainty strutted in, a peacock so proud,
But behind it lurked chaos, not one to be cowed.
Thought I had plans, all neatly in line,
Then tripped on my shoelaces, lost track of time.

With a checklist in hand, I marched to the beat,
Only to find my shoes were on my feet.
The universe chuckled, a mischievous friend,
Said, "Surprise! Here's a twist at the end!"

Caught in the act of my grand misdirection,
I laughed at the dance of this wild connection.
When certainty met its quirky surprise,
Life turned into comedy beneath the wide skies.

So here's to the moments that turn plans to jest,
When routine's a riddle, and chaos is best.
With a wink and a grin, I'll take a wild ride,
In the carnival chaos, let laughter abide.

Unraveling the Threads of Belief

Oh, the tapestry woven with threads of the known,
Loomed with the tales of the seeds I had sown.
But tugging on yarns that seemed ever so tight,
Brought forth a dance in the pale moonlight.

Each stitch I had made in the fabric of dreams,
Kept fraying and fraying at the seams.
So I pranced with the doubts, a jig in my heart,
Finding joy in the chaos, a bizarre kind of art.

Beliefs unraveled like socks in the wash,
Confusion erupted, a whimsical squash.
Every knot in the thread was a giggle and fate,
Unraveling wonders, hilarious bait.

So let's toast to the tangle that life can bestow,
A joyful disaster, a comical show.
In the threads of uncertainty, I'll craft my own mold,
With humor my guide, I'll be brave, I'll be bold.

The Landscape of Uncertainty

In a world of logic, I took a stand,
Plans all mapped out, just like I planned.
But the roads seemed to twist, oh what a surprise,
Turns out my GPS just opened its eyes.

With maps in hand and a confident grin,
I set out to win, oh where to begin?
But clouds had a laugh, they forgot to clear,
And my compass pointed south, much to my fear.

I packed all the snacks, the usual fare,
For every adventure, a feast to prepare.
Yet the picnic I laid turned into a race,
As ants hosted parties and stole my space.

So here in this land of the topsy-turvy,
I embrace the odd laugh, the path that's unworthy.
For certainty's a myth, just like unicorns,
But I'll dance with confusion and toast to my scorns.

Waking from the Dream of Certainty

I woke up one day feeling mighty bold,
With dreams tightly wrapped in a blanket of gold.
But a sock on my shoe and a cat on my head,
Told me that certainty slept with the dead.

With coffee in hand and a plan in my mind,
I strut through the door, hoping life would be kind.
But a pigeon appeared, it stole my last fry,
Guess even the birds are in on this lie.

I skipped down the sidewalk like I was on air,
Only to trip, fall, and lose quite a share.
Of dignity, grace, and my brand-new shoe,
But laughter was all that I really could do.

So here's to the mornings we start without a clue,
Where certainty's absent and mirth feels so true.
I'll wear mismatched socks, take a twirl and a prance,
For life without structure is still worth the dance.

Through the Lens of Unpredictability

I bought a new camera to capture my flair,
Pulled the trigger quick, and it bounced in mid-air.
With pictures of pigeons and squirrels doing flips,
It seems the lens knew more about other folks' trips.

With every snap taken, a joke's in the frame,
The world insists on playing a silly game.
A dog wore a hat, a cat played the drums,
While I just stood back, shaking my thumbs.

Off to the park with a bucket of dreams,
Only to find my sandwich lost to the streams.
A curious duck took a liking to bread,
While I tried to explain it's my lunch that's now fed.

So here's to the moments we try to preserve,
Through the lens of a world that refuses to serve.
Let's laugh at the chaos, and cheer on the jest,
For uncertainty's selfie is truly the best.

When Knowledge Became an Enigma

I opened a book, oh what a delight,
Knowledge awaited at the edge of the light.
Yet every word danced, like a choreographed fable,
And my mind played the role of an unwilling label.

I scribbled some notes, random thoughts came alive,
But thought one plus one somehow equaled five.
With equations all tangled like a bowl of spaghetti,
My brain had a party, but lost the confetti.

They say knowledge is power; oh what a tease,
It turned into riddles that brought me to my knees.
With puzzles and riddles, my head started to spin,
While my cat just rolled over, oblivious to win.

So here's to the quest where I fumble and flail,
Chasing down wisdom on a runaway trail.
When knowledge confuses, I dance like a fool,
Embracing the laughter that brightens the school.

The Silence After the Storm

After chaos, a calm seems near,
But my sock's gone, oh dear!
The cat's now king of the chair,
While I'm stuck in my own nightmare.

Rainbows smile, but my hair's a fright,
The dog got muddy; what a sight!
Lost my keys, where could they be?
Guess the universe is playing tricks on me.

The winds howl, my plans scatter wide,
That pizza I ordered has nowhere to hide!
Fluffy clouds float in blissful frown,
As I trip on a shoe and land on the ground.

Yet through the laughter in disarray,
Life's quirks dance in their own ballet.
I'll twirl with pain, a silly feat,
Guess tomorrow I'll hope for a little less heat.

The Sifting Sand of Assumption

I thought my cake was all baked right,
But it collapsed; oh, what a sight!
When life hands you crumbs, bake again,
And hope for some sweet little gain.

At the beach, I lost my shoes,
Sand between my toes gives me the blues.
The sun beats down like clockwork fun,
Turning my thoughts to how I've spun.

Mistakes piled high, like summer sand,
Swirling 'round like it's all unplanned.
Next trip might just be to the park,
Where the only surprise is a barking lark.

But hey, laughter tickles the air,
As I fumble about without a care.
With each misplaced step, a jest to share,
I'll dance on the beach like the seagulls dare!

Shadowlands of the Uncertain Heart

In shadows lurk my wildest dreams,
That turn to dust, or so it seems.
Last night's plan? Gone with the breeze,
Now I'm debating my new car keys.

In the dark, I missed my shoe,
And walked right into a chair or two.
My heart beats fast, but it's all for show,
When did my life become a bizarre show?

Each decision's like a puppet on strings,
Dancing around with silly things.
Should I wear blue or opt for red?
Perhaps go straighter instead of misled?

So here I stand, quite unsure,
Like a cat that ponders 'what's the lure?'
But deep down inside, I know it's fine,
Just a jester's life, all wrapped in rhyme.

Chronicles of Disenchantment

Once I thought the world was bright,
But now I battle with loads of fright.
The toast burned black; my coffee's cold,
Life's twists and turns are like tales of old.

Oh, the laundry that piled high in a heap,
A mountain of clothes just won't let me sleep!
They say, 'Sort it out!' like that's the charm,
But all I feel is laundry alarm.

Plans laid out like a careful map,
All went sideways; oh, what a trap!
Dinner's a disaster, and cats rule the roost,
Yet somehow, I manage — a strange little boost.

Still, I stroll through this quirky maze,
With my heart on my sleeve, caught in a daze.
Life's a circus, a funny old ride,
And in laughter, I find my curious pride.

When Plans Collide with Reality

I woke up with a scheme in mind,
A playlist of success I thought I'd find.
But coffee spilled across my notes,
Now I'm lost in my own silly quotes.

I dashed off to the store to buy,
A dozen eggs, oh me, oh my!
The cart flipped over, eggs took flight,
Now I've got a breakfast, but not quite right.

I mapped out roads of joy and glee,
Yet ended up in a tree, oh me!
My GPS, it laughed and smiled,
Who needs a trail when laughter's wild?

In the grand design of life's parade,
Turns out, spontaneity's the upgrade.
I once had plans like a well-formed letter,
But hey, who knew that chaos is better?

A Garden of Doubt Blossoms

In my backyard, I planted seeds,
Imagined blooms, fulfilling needs.
But what sprouted was quite a sight,
A jungle of weeds that felt just right.

With watering can, I took my stand,
Dreaming of flowers, perfectly planned.
But dandelions waved, and oh dear,
They cheered my gardening, loud and clear!

I pruned with hope, a clumsy task,
With shorts and shades, I dared to ask.
Where are the daisies, the lovely pansies?
Instead, I've got a haven for fake mancies.

Now every time I see a bloom,
I remember my ambitious doom.
In this garden of doubt, I do abide,
With laughter intertwined in nature's tide.

The Struggle Between Knowing and Being

I thought I knew the secret to life,
Like a chef with a knife, managing strife.
But every recipe turned to goo,
My dinner guests turned to 'who's who?'

In pondering paths of wise men past,
I found myself at a gentle cast.
Should I dance like nobody's there?
Or just sit still in my old armchair?

With books stacked high, I took a leap,
Into the wisdom that had me sleep.
Each quote misquoted, was it fate?
Or just a funny twist on my plate?

In this dance between thought and deed,
Turns out, my heart's the funniest breed.
For knowing's a puzzle, so neat and sly,
I laugh and grin, just asking why.

Horizons of Unfathomable Mystery

I gazed out at the distant view,
Hoping clarity would come into view.
Yet clouds rolled in, a comedic shroud,
All I saw was what I doubted aloud.

Maps and charts lined my coffee stain,
Exploring wonders, yes, I'd entertain.
But every road led back to me,
Wandering lost, like a bumblebee.

With every question, more appeared,
Horizons stretched, but wise men sneered.
What if the truth is just a joke,
And we're all players in a grand poke?

So here I stand, my compass lost,
Navigating humor at any cost.
In horizons wide, I must agree,
Life's best adventures are yet to be.

The Art of Unraveling Expectations

My plans were set, like shoes on feet,
A dance with certainty, oh so sweet.
But then a shoe flew off the stage,
And laughter blasted like a sage.

I spoke of futures, bold and bright,
While juggling dreams by day and night.
But every promise took a dive,
And now I'm in a clown's beehive.

With maps and charts, I drew my way,
Yet found a detour on display.
I brought a compass, trusty, true,
It pointed right—then said, "Boo-hoo!"

In the art of plans, a masterpiece,
Where chaos reigns, I find my peace.
So here I am, a jovial sort,
Navigating life like a funny sport.

Searching for Solace in the Chaos

In a world of mess, I sought a seat,
Tangled in laughter, can't find my feet.
Worries piled high, like dirty socks,
In the hustle, wear mismatched clocks.

I searched for silence, a tranquil pond,
But found instead, a rubbery bond.
Each answer slipped like soap in hand,
While chaos giggled, oh so grand.

Tried to catch calm, like a fleeting dream,
But it danced away—what a silly scheme!
Chased it in circles, around the bend,
While the jokes just doubled, around the trend.

In the thick of storm, I twirl and spin,
With a pie in my face, let the day begin.
Searching for solace—what a great tease,
Life's chaos, it seems, just aims to please!

The Day the Answers Evaporated

I woke one morning, bright and keen,
  Hoping for clarity, crisp and clean.
But answers fled like dandelion seeds,
  Leaving behind a field of weeds.

With coffee in hand and notes in a stack,
I searched for brilliance—that little knack.
  Yet each solution slipped my grip,
  Like trying to hold water on a trip.

I called out, "Hey, where'd you go?"
But doubt just giggled, "I'm the show!"
  And every theory took a detour,
Leaving me with riddles, that's for sure.

Then suddenly, laughter burst through the wall,
As I stumbled and fumbled, tripping on a call.
The day was wacky, yet pointedly bright,
Where answers vanished but the fun stayed in sight.

Unraveling the Fabric of Assumptions

I wove a tapestry, bright and bold,
With threads of certainty, or so I was told.
But one little tug, and what did I find?
A string of confusion, oddly entwined.

Each fabric whisper spoke up loud,
Saying, "Expectations? You're far too proud!"
My patterns frayed, with laughter, applause,
As I unraveled my dreams without a cause.

I stitched together what I believed,
But holes appeared that I couldn't achieve.
Now it's patchwork, a jumbled delight,
With colors clashing, yet feeling so right.

In this quirky quilt, I dance and twirl,
Where every thread tells a different swirl.
Unraveling assumptions—a game I adore,
In the fabric of life, I find room to explore.

Getting Lost in the Details

In a world of lists, I wrote my plans,
Yet forgot my keys, oh the silly jams.
A map in one hand, snacks in the other,
Who knew that coffee would lead to a bother?

Numbers and letters dance in my brain,
Counted my steps, but forgot the train.
With every turn, another new twist,
Lost in the details, my list I missed.

Bagon and fog, the town I seek,
Instead found a cat, looking sleek.
It guided me home, with a lazy stare,
I followed its path, just to see where.

Laughter erupted, fate played its part,
Stumbled through life with a half-broken heart.
Joy in the chaos, a twist of the plot,
Lessons unlearned, yet still I forgot.

The False Horizon Revealed

Chasing the sunset, a race against time,
Thought I had a plan, so perfectly prime.
But the road, it twisted, then vanished from sight,
Turns out the horizon just loves to delight.

Like a mirage seen on a hot summer day,
That promise of rest seems to drift away.
With every new bend, the views were a tease,
I labelled it progress, but laughed with unease.

Friends on the couch said, 'Stay right on track!',
But they all fell asleep, so I went for a snack.
Plans turned to snacks, with giggles galore,
Turns out my journey was just quite a chore.

Next time I venture and chase the sun down,
I'll bring a map, and maybe a frown.
For laughter is better than plans in a purse,
Embrace the absurd or get lost in reverse.

What Lies Beneath the Surface

Peeking through the pond, I saw my delight,
A glittering fish, oh what a sight!
But when I leaned closer, it leapt with a splash,
Just a charming prank, such a quick flash.

Underneath the calm, the chaos will brew,
The ripples of laughter seeping through too.
Ah, the wisdom that bubbles right up to your chin,
Life laughs aloud when you think you will win.

Diving too deep, what treasures I seek,
Only found mud, rearranged and unique.
Searching for answers in a puddle so clear,
Turns out it's just memories, my biggest fear.

Now I chuckle, the rock left unturned,
For wisdom and humor are lessons well learned.
When life pulls a prank, just play along,
And dance with the fish to a playful song.

Beneath the Weight of Assumptions

Stacking my thoughts like blocks on a shelf,
Each one a treasure, or so I tell myself.
When they teeter and fall, it's quite a loud crash,
Turns out my grand plan was not meant to last.

With every assumption, a tower I build,
Hoping for wisdom that remains unfulfilled.
But under the rubble, I see something bright,
Laughter and joy, my ultimate light.

Judging my journey, based on what's seen,
Ignoring the beauty that lies in between.
A lesson found buried in all of my mess,
Laughter's the key, it's simply the best.

With each heavy guess, I stumble and sway,
Beneath all the weight, find the fun in the fray.
So here's to the journey, messy and sweet,
Where laughter's the treasure, and joy is the treat.

Beneath the Fabric of Understanding

Woke up one day, my plans in a row,
But socks in the dryer just won't flow.
A map in my hand, I think I see clear,
Turns out it points to the fridge, oh dear.

I plotted my course like a captain bold,
With GPS skills that I say are gold.
Yet the right turn I missed made me lose my way,
Now I'm asking a barista, can I stay?

Coffee in hand, still feeling confused,
Post-it notes everywhere, gathering dust.
I promise next week I'll have it all straight,
But today I'll just eat a cupcake on fate.

Laughter surrounds me as chaos reigns,
As I juggle life's puzzles and silly refrains.
Maybe life's plan is just ghastly fun,
With socks and cupcakes, we've already won.

The Silent Reckoning of Choices Made.

In my bubble of wisdom, I float with glee,
Choices secure like a fresh-brewed cup of tea.
But the laundry's a monster, it silently bides,
To wear mismatched socks is one of life's guides.

I enrolled in a class to master the art,
Of cooking and baking, where do I start?
The cake fell flat, an architectural feat,
Turns out flour and water don't make a treat.

Now the markers are scattered, plans on a page,
Doodles of nonsense, life's funny stage.
I play the lead role in this grand charade,
With stand-up routines as my dreams fade.

Friends laugh and tease, their laughter is sweet,
As I ponder my next culinary feat.
But in the end, I'll just snack while I smile,
For it's all in the journey, let's stay for a while.

Beyond the Illusion of Certainty

I crafted a master plan, a fine ballet,
Each step choreographed, hip-hip hooray!
But the cat on the counter, with flour on paws,
Has declared an uprising without any flaws.

With confidence high, I chose my attire,
A shirt mismatched, but hey, who's a liar?
I strutted outside like I owned the street,
Till a neighbor pointed at my mismatched feet.

The time was set for a grand evening feast,\nYet the oven had chosen to prank like a beast.
With smoke on the rise, I waved it away,
Turns out it was just dinner's 'surprise' ballet.

The laughter erupts, and glasses they clink,
As I shake off the stress and ponder a drink.
In the chaos of life, let joy keep us near,
Even when we're lost, it's all good cheer.

Chasing Shadows of Understanding

In pursuit of the truth, I danced in the light,
With visions of clarity shining so bright.
But the glasses I wore were decidedly wrong,
Now I'm in the shadows, hum-humming a song.

A morning routine that I thought was clever,
Turns out I've been nesting with pillows, however.
Waking up late, I missed half the day,
While socks soaked in coffee just laugh in dismay.

I scribble my goals on a napkin of dreams,
Yet life's little hiccups aren't always as they seem.
A scatter of chaos, a dash of ping-pong,
Is this the right path, or is it all wrong?

So toast to the mishaps, the fun we create,
For stumbling through life is a wonderful fate.
We'll chuckle through life with our mismatched shoes,
Realizing the wisdom in all that we choose.

The Fragile Thread of Belief

With plans laid out like cards on the floor,
I danced through life, an open door.
But fate shuffled hands, emotions went wild,
And logic retreated like a lost child.

My compass spun wildly, north became south,
Thoughts tumbled like bubbles straight out of my mouth.
Each turn was a giggle, each step a mistake,
I laughed at the chaos, for laughter's at stake.

Like a juggler fumbling with one too many balls,
I chased every answer, but tumbled through halls.
Reality tickled and pulled at my seams,
As bewilderment wrapped me in whimsical dreams.

And when clarity peeked through the fog I had made,
I waved it goodbye; who needs to be played?
For life's a grand circus, all joy with a frown,
And I'm just the clown with my life upside down.

When Certainty Became a Stranger

I strutted with pride, like a king in his throne,
With every bold step, I thought I'd outgrown.
But the ground slipped away; what a slippery joke!
As certainty chuckled, then vanished in smoke.

Each wise choice I made was a shot in the dark,
Like playing the banjo in the deep of a park.
My map turned to riddles, each road led to woe,
But oh, all the laughs! What a delightful show!

Friends gathered around, they just couldn't believe,
How each grand adventure was hard to conceive.
As questions piled up, like dishes left lingering,
I threw up my hands, the fun just keeps swinging!

So here's to the times when I thought I was right,
When certainty waltzed off into the night.
With a wink and a grin, I'll dance on this stage,
For life's silly twists are the best on the page.

Illusions Woven in Confidence

With threads of ambition, I crafted my fate,
Each stitch was so sure, oh, I felt so great.
But as I wove dreams in a tapestry bright,
The fabric unraveled, oh what a sight!

I donned my best smile, ready to win,
But crafted illusions turned watery thin.
They floated like bubbles, then popped with a *plop*,
Leaving laughter behind, as I learned how to flop.

I was convinced I could juggle the stars,
Yet here I am, standing with plenty of scars.
Each plan turned to jests, a relatable scene,
As I spun in circles, feeling quite keen.

But what a delight in this messy charade,
Where folly is gold, and wrinkles are laid.
So I'll toast to the times every vision did flop,
For joy's in the laughter each blunder fills up!

The Mask of Complacency Unveiled

A mask of contentment, so safely I wore,
With comforts surrounding, who could ask for more?
But reality chuckled, a sly little sprite,
And pulled off my mask in the dead of the night.

My comfort zone trembled, like jelly on plates,
As new twists and turns danced at my gates.
Like a cat with nine lives just pawing for fun,
I twirled in confusion, while life played its pun.

With every faux pas, I stumbled and fell,
Disguised in my laughter, you couldn't quite tell.
Yet wisdom danced in, all silly and spry,
And I learned that the "known" can sometimes just lie.

So here's to the moments when life wears a grin,
And old masks of comfort are chucked in the bin.
With folly, I march into the great unknown,
For laughter's the treasure that makes it my own!

Realizations in the Silence of Reflection

In the mirror, a smile so wide,
Yet inside, a rollercoaster ride.
My plans all set, like shoes untied,
How do I navigate this bumpy tide?

The coffee's cold, my mind's a whirl,
I chase my thoughts like a tumbleweed twirl.
With wisdom gained from a pirate's pearl,
Can I steer this ship, or just watch it unfurl?

A map in hand, and directions wrong,
I hum a tune that's just too long.
Each step I take, I trip and throng,
Sailing on seas where I don't belong.

Yet laughter echoes in every doubt,
Like clowns in a circus, having a rout.
With every twist and a comedic pout,
I find the joy in what life's about.

Charting the Waters of Doubt

With a compass broken and no clear map,
I sail through waters that feel like a trap.
Fish tales told, but I'm in a flap,
Lost in the currents, a nautical gap.

The captain's hat, a gift from my cat,
Advice so wise, but where's the chat?
Waves of worries, and I can't adapt,
Each splash feels like a slap on the mat.

Oceans of chaos, I laugh in surprise,
Navigating storms with unsteady ties.
In this wild ride, I wear no disguise,
Just bobbing along, beneath cloudy skies.

Yet here I am, with a grin so wide,
Charting this chaos like a joyful ride.
For in this mess, I can't help but glide,
A captain of blunders, and full of pride.

The Veil of Simplicity Lifted

Lift the curtain, oh what a sight,
Things aren't simple, but that's alright.
Like making toast with a fruit fight,
My breakfast plans have taken flight!

A recipe book, a mystery novel,
I mix and mash, then find a bobble.
In clever mix-ups, there's always trouble,
Cooking's a craft, but it's a puzzle.

With spatulas flying and eggs on the floor,
I try to create but end up with more.
Each mishap laughs while I implore,
What's cooking here? What's in store?

Yet through the chaos, I find my groove,
The best meals come with a wild move.
In kitchen dramas, I start to prove,
Simplicity's veil? Oh, I disapprove!

Lighthouses in the Fog of Confusion

In the fog, a flicker, a beam shines bright,
But is it a lighthouse or just a light?
I row my boat, chasing the sight,
Wondering if I'm wrong or right.

Waves of laughter crash with a roar,
Directions change like a mischievous chore.
Each buoy I spot makes me want to explore,
But all I find are jokes at the shore.

With seagulls laughing, the tides are a jest,
I follow the rhythm, I aim for the best.
In between lines, I might just rest,
Finding comedy in an awkward quest.

So here I float, in the mist I grin,
Navigating life with a good-natured spin.
For in this confusion, where do I begin?
With laughter as my compass, I'm bound to win!

When the Puzzle Pieces Refused to Fit

I gathered pieces with great flair,
Colors bright, and shapes that dare.
But one was round, and one was square,
My masterpiece? A puzzle nightmare!

With every twist, a giggle grew,
A cat's ear here, a duck's foot too.
I laughed so hard, I nearly blew,
The cat meowed, "What's wrong with you?"

Friends gathered 'round to lend a hand,
We aimed for order, but it was planned.
Two pieces stuck, oh isn't it grand?
The final shape, a lopsided land!

We celebrated with pizza feast,
A victory dance, to say the least.
Though puzzles failed, our spirits increased,
In chaos, we found joy released!

The Weight of Unfulfilled Promises

I bought a gym pass, thought I'd be fit,
Dreams of six-pack abs, not a single bit.
But couch and snacks won each little skit,
Now my weight's a true fitness wit!

Promises made in the mirror's gleam,
"Tomorrow I'll start!" was my bright theme.
Yet here I lie, in a donut dream,
Life's too short, or so it would seem!

In workout gear, I look quite fly,
But those weights stare back with a sigh.
To lift or not, oh me, oh my,
Maybe next week? Wait, sounds like a lie!

So here I sit, guilt on my plate,
Binge-watching shows while I contemplate.
With laughter and snacks, I celebrate,
In the weight of dreams, I'm comfortably late!

Confronting the Mirage of Certainty

In a world of maps and clear-cut lines,
I thought I knew all the grand designs.
Yet signs pointed, and crossed my signs,
   Making plans feel like jigsaw rhymes.

With every step, the ground would slip,
   Confidence riding a fanciful trip.
Each 'should' became a stumbling quip,
   Around every corner, a comedy flip!

I scribbled rules, oh so quaint,
Then tripped on laughter, fell like a saint.
Turns out, chaos is what we paint,
A dance of questions, we mustn't faint!

With every wrong turn, I learned to play,
The questions dance, they lead the way.
In the joke of life, we'll sway and stay,
   For certainty's mirage leads us astray!

In the Shadows of My Obsession

In the dark of night, I paced, I yearned,
For tidiness around, a corner turned.
Obsessed with clean, my thoughts all churned,
A sock misplaced? Oh, how I burned!

I labeled jars, I sorted every shoe,
Each item missed, a horror show anew.
But chaos chuckled, as if it knew,
That order's facade wouldn't stick like glue.

My closet laughed, a comical ghost,
Outfits laughed back at my careful boast.
I swore to conquer, be the perfect host,
But clutter's charm? Now that's a toast!

In my neat-freak mission, I found amusement,
Lost in the mess, a joyous confusion.
In the shadows danced my sweet delusion,
Embracing chaos? Now, that's the fusion!

Embracing the Unknown

Life's maze twists and turns our way,
Like socks that vanish, lead us astray.
With each step forward, the backtrack's a dance,
Stumbling on joy in a game of chance.

Plans made in pen turn to doodles in chalk,
Maps lead to nowhere, let's take a walk.
When GPS says 'left' and it's just a tree,
I laugh at the wonders that won't set me free.

Pizza for dinner, or maybe a stew?
Decisions so hard, like which shoe to chew.
Uncertainty's here with its winks and its grins,
I roll with the punches; it's where life begins.

The future's a jester with tricks up its sleeve,
A pie chart of laughs that we all must believe.
So let's toast to the chaos, the wobbly ride,
With friends by my side, there's no need to hide.

The Echoes of What Was Once Clear

Once a map was drawn, marked with flair,
It showed the way, or so we'd declare.
Directions so certain, they sparked much delight,
Now ghosts of confusion come dance in the light.

Remember the time when we knew every score?
Now trivia questions leave us wanting more.
The answers escaped like a cat on the run,
Chasing our tails, oh what wit we've won!

Those grand aspirations now seem rather absurd,
Like asking a cow about lines in a herd.
What once felt like life's prompting applause,
Now giggles at wisdom's far more silly flaws.

Yet in every blunder, humor finds place,
Life's like a joke, full of smiles and grace.
So I'll wear mismatched socks, and let laughter out,
For clarity's overrated, this life's what it's about.

A Puzzle Missing Vital Pieces

A jigsaw of life, missing parts at the start,
Pieces all jumbled, they refuse to depart.
Look here and look there, frustration grows wide,
Yet giggles arise as I chuck them aside.

The corners were solid, the edges were neat,
Now colors collide in a baffling feat.
With old instructions lost, I just sorta guess,
Like finding a unicorn in fancy dress!

Oh, where is the piece that looks just like a cat?
Searching for wisdom amidst all this spat.
Sipping confusion like brew from a mug,
Every missed puzzle brings forth a new shrug.

Laughter is treasure when things go askew,
Turn every chaos to something that's true.
So I'll dance with the puzzle that cannot complete,
Finding joy in the edges, and life's funny beat.

Tides of Certainty and Uncertainty

Life's tides pull back, and then crash with a swell,
What seemed like a tale, now a riddle to tell.
Once sure like a rock, now I drift like the foam,
Navigating waves that don't feel like home.

Plans washed away, they float out to sea,
Still, I grab on tight to what's funny and free.
With nets full of laughter, I cast to the shore,
Collecting the moments, unsure of what's more.

A boat made of whimsy, I sail through the fog,
Avoiding the missteps, like a petulant dog.
Every bob and a weave, I wear like a crown,
With sands shifting under, I'll never drown.

For amidst all the chaos, there's joy to be found,
It's the splashes of silly that truly astound.
So I'll battle the tides with my own brand of cheer,
In this sea of confusion, I'll steer and persevere.

www.ingramcontent.com/pod-product-compliance
Lightning Source LLC
Chambersburg PA
CBHW051637160426
43209CB00004B/679